MY BODY'S MINE

A Book on Boundaries and Sexual Abuse Prevention

by

KAYLA J. W. MARNACH

With a foreword by:
JESSICA KILPATRICK, M.A., LPC

Illustrated by Kate Swinney

YANA Press

My Body's Mine

A Book on Boundaries and Sexual Abuse Prevention

Printed in the United States of America

YANA Press
Austin, Texas

CanDoKidsSeries.com

FOREWORD

My Body's Mine is an excellent book for both parents and professionals alike. This book was created with the goal of educating children about boundaries and sexual abuse in a way that is empowering and encouraging. Parents often worry that talking about sexual abuse will cause their child to have unnecessary fears and worries. Parents want their children to be safe, but they are often uncomfortable and intimidated when it comes to broaching the subject. This book gives parents a simple and playful way to allow their child to listen and then ask questions. My Body's Mine gives children ownership of their body and teaches them they have the right to say no and to go and tell a safe adult.

I encourage medical and mental health professionals to use this book with clients. I have found it particularly helpful with children who have been through abuse to encourage them for being brave and telling an adult what happened. Clients can learn their rights and that they did not do anything wrong. Through the use of this book, I have experienced families being able to openly discuss abuse together for the first time.

Kayla Marnach's heart for children from hard places is infectious. Her vision for all children to know they are not alone is unfolding in this new book. She is a gifted writer who will continue to create works benefiting children. My Body's Mine was a missing piece of literature in abuse prevention and I am so thankful to Kayla for writing it!

Jessica Kilpatrick, M.A., LPC

STARRY

DEDICATION

Every person has the right to control what happens to his or her body. Life is diminished when that right is taken away, but it doesn't have to stay that way. Each moment is filled with choices, but we need informed choices. We need to know our rights, because our choice in any given situation determines the impact it has on our life.

This book is dedicated to every child, every *person* empowering them to take charge of the precious body and life they have been given, to lead it to the fullest with joy.

MY BODY'S MINE

My body's mine
From neck to knee,
And no one's free
To be touching me.

From head to toe,
My body's mine.
I love my body
And it's all mine.

Hugs are okay

If I say so,

But I am free

To tell them, "No!"

Kiss my cheek

Might be okay,

But only if

I say you may.

A safe grownup

Will never say,

"Don't dare tell

What we did today."

And if they do,

I'm going to yell.

I'm going to run.

I'm going to tell.

A yucky feeling
Is good to know
My body's saying,
"It's time to go!"

"It's time to leave!
Get out of there!
Go tell someone
You know will care."

10

My body's mine
From neck to knee,
And no one's free
To be touching me.

From head to toe,
My body's mine.
I love my body
And it's all mine.

A safe grownup
Is someone who
Will listen to me,
Knows what to do.

A safe grownup
Will take my side,
They never hurt
Or make me hide.

A mom, or teacher,
A sister or friend
Should keep me safe.
Me, they defend.

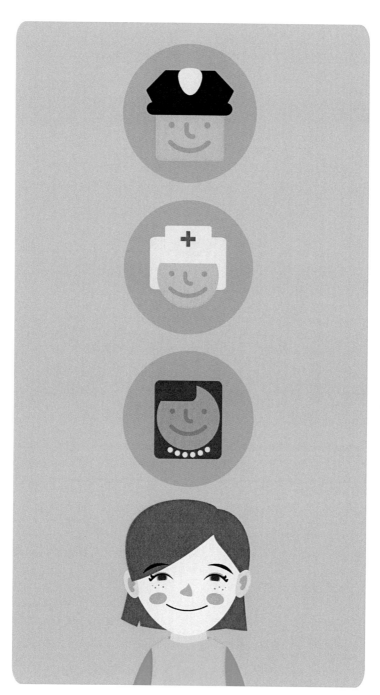

But if they don't,
I'm going to yell.
I'm going to run.
I'm going to tell!

And I won't stop
Until they know
To keep me safe
Wherever I go.

A safe grownup
Keeps me from harm.
If I've been touched
They sound the alarm.

My body's mine
From neck to knee,
And no one's free
To be touching me.

From head to toe,
My body's mine.
I love my body
And it's all mine.

QUESTIONS AND EXPLORATIONS

1. In the book, they say you can tell someone "no" if they touch your body in a way that you do not like. Can you show me with a big voice how you can tell someone, "No!"

2. How did you feel when you yelled, "No!"?

3. Why can you tell them, "No!"?

4. What is something a safe grownup will never say?

5. How do you think the little boy feels when the adult tells him to keep a secret?

6. What do you tell someone who says they want you to keep secrets?

7. Who could you go and tell?

8. What would you say to a friend if they tell you an adult told them to keep a secret?

9. What would you do if a friend told you to keep it a secret?

10. Who would you go and tell?

11. Why would you go and tell?

12. How do you think the little girl is feeling when she's holding her stomach?

13. Have you ever had a yucky feeling?

14. What happened to make you feel yucky?

15. Did you tell someone about your yucky feeling?

16. How did it feel to talk about it?

17. If you get a yucky feeling again, what can you do?

18. How do you think the little girl feels when she tells someone safe?

19. How do you think you would feel?

20. How many people can you name that are safe to tell?

21. Why are they safe?

22. If someone you think is safe doesn't help you, what do you do?

23. Who would you tell?

24. How would you tell them?

ABOUT THE AUTHOR

A native Texan, Kayla lives with her husband and three cats in Austin. Her two married daughters, along with her faith, have been an inspiration in many of her writings. She has been a guest speaker at elementary schools, women's retreats, writer's groups, and University of Texas. At the request of teachers and counselors, she has provided stories to broach difficult situations. Her passion is to empower and validate children, helping them know they are not alone in their feelings or circumstance, and ways to deal with it. When she is not writing she loves spending time with family and friends, read, scrapbook, and watch old movies.

ABOUT THE ILLUSTRATOR

From Austin, Texas, Kate is a young, up and coming artist and designer studying at Abilene Christian University. She loves integrating art with technology to make beautiful designs. In the future Kate intends to continue to pursue digital illustration along with many other fields of design. In her spare time she enjoys music and food of all varieties. She is inspired by the profoundly talented professors at the University and her greatest love, Armando Collazo.

For Other Books in the Can Do Kids Series Visit

CanDoKidsSeries.com

Made in the USA
San Bernardino, CA
09 December 2017